SILLY SOUP!

Written by
KATE RUTTLE

Illustrated by
SANDRA AGUILLAR

WAYLAND

First published in 2011
by Wayland

This paperback edition published
in 2012 by Wayland

Wayland
338 Euston Road
London NW1 3BH

Wayland Australia
Level 17/207 Kent Street
Sydney, NSW 2000

Series editor: Louise John
Designer: Paul Cherrill
Consultant: Kate Ruttle

A CIP catalogue record for this book is available
from the British Library.

ISBN 9780750266512

Printed in China

Wayland is a division of Hachette Children's Books,
an Hachette UK company. www.hachette.co.uk

FiZZ WiZZ PHONiCS is a series of fun and exciting books, especially designed to be used by children who have not yet started to read.

The books support the development of language, exploring key speaking and listening skills, as well as encouraging confidence in pre-reading skills.

SILLY SOUP! is all about rhythm and rhyme. This book includes a selection of well-known songs and nursery rhymes that children will have fun joining in with. As children sing along they will become familiar with different rhythms, developing an awareness of rhythm and rhyme in speech.

For suggestions on how to use **SILLY SOUP!** and for further activities, look at page 24 of this book.

Humpty Dumpty

Humpty Dumpty sat on a wall.
Humpty Dumpty had a great fall.

All the king's horses,
and all the king's men,
couldn't put Humpty together again.

Buckle My Shoe

One, two, buckle my shoe.
Three, four, knock at the door.

Five, six, pick up sticks.
Seven, eight, lay them straight.
Nine, ten, a big fat hen.

Twinkle, Twinkle

Twinkle twinkle little star,
how I wonder what you are.
Up above the world so high,
like a diamond in the sky.

Twinkle twinkle little star,
how I wonder what you are.

Jack and Jill

Jack and Jill
went up the hill,
to fetch a pail of water.

Jack fell down
and broke his crown,
and Jill came tumbling after.

Little Bo-Peep

Little Bo-Peep has lost her sheep,
and doesn't know where to find them.

Leave them alone,
and they'll come home,
wagging their tails behind them.

Incy Wincy Spider

Incy Wincy Spider
climbed up the water spout.
Down came the rain,
and washed the spider out.

Out came the sunshine,
and dried up all the rain.
So Incy Wincy Spider
climbed up the spout again.

Hey Diddle, Diddle

Hey diddle, diddle,
the cat and the fiddle.
The cow jumped over the moon.

The little dog laughed
to see such sport,
and the dish ran away with the spoon.

Old King Cole

Old King Cole was a merry old soul,
and a merry old soul was he.

He called for his pipe,
and he called for his bowl,
and he called for his fiddlers three.

Three Blind Mice

Three blind mice,
three blind mice,
see how they run!
See how they run!

They all run after the farmer's wife,
who cut off their tails with a carving knife.
Did ever you see such a thing in your life,
as three blind mice?

Silly Soup!

I'm making lots of silly soup,
I'm making soup that's silly.
I'm going to cook it in the fridge,
to make it nice and chilly.

In goes:
A fox, a box, some socks.
A train, some rain, a chain.
A tree, a bee, a key.

Further Activities

These activities can be used when reading the book one-to-one, or in the home.

These activities can be used when using the book with more than one child, or in an educational setting.

P4 • Sing the nursery rhyme until you are familiar with it. Then try and sing the song without looking at the page.

P6 • Look carefully at the picture. Can you see anything that rhymes with 'two' and 'shoe'? How about something that rhymes with 'ten' and 'hen'? Try to think of things to rhyme with other numbers, too.

P8 • Sing the song until you are familiar with it. Can you hear any rhyming words in the song?

P10 • Walk around the room while you sing the first verse of this rhyme. Can you walk in time to the beat of the song?

P12 • Little Bo-Peep has lost her sheep. Can you find them for her in the picture? Can you see a word in the rhyme that rhymes with 'Peep'?

P14 • Act out the rhyme while you sing it. Can you feel the skipping beat of the syllables? For example IN-cy WIN-cy SPI-DER, climbed UP the WA-ter SPOUT.

P16 • Find some household objects, such as toy animals, spoons and dishes and try to act out the song.
• Can your hear any rhyming words in the song? Can you find any rhyming words in the picture?

P18 • Sing the song and think about the objects in the rhyme. Can you see any other objects in the picture that rhyme with 'king'?

P20 • Listen carefully to the song as you sing it. Talk about the repetition of the first lines and the fact that the rhythm speeds up a lot after those lines are complete.

P22 • Sing the song and think about the objects in the rhyme. Can you find any other objects in the picture which rhyme with the words in the verse?
• Can you think of any other kinds of rhyming soup? For example a fish, a dish, a wish; a coat, a boat, a goat.

P4 • Have a look at the illustration on the page. Can you find an object in the artwork which rhymes with 'wall' and fall' and another which rhymes with 'men'? Talk about the rationale for the rhyming decisions.

P6 • Find pictures of a shoe, a door, some sticks and a hen. Repeat the rhyme, stopping before the word each time. Can you identify which of your pictures is needed to fill in the gaps? Talk about why.

P8 • Look at the illustration on the page. Can you find an object in the picture which rhymes with 'star'?

P10 • Use percussion instruments and try to keep the beat while you sing the song. Focus on the first verse only.

P12 • Find a video clip of children singing the nursery rhyme on the Internet. Join in with the song.
• Can you find the rhyming words in the nursery rhyme?

P14 • Play the music or find the song on the Internet. Join in with the music, clapping and singing the song at the same time. Talk about the claps. Are they all the same weight?

P16 • Sing the song, focusing on the rhyming words 'moon' and 'spoon'. If the cow jumped over a star, what might the dish run away with? What if it was the Sun or a cloud?

P18 • Find some pictures of a pipe, a bowl and a fiddler on the Internet. Can you point to the correct object in your pictures as you sing the nursery rhyme?

P20 • Move around the room while you sing the rhyme. Stamp your feet to match the rhythm. What happens to your stamps when you get to the second verse? Are you running as fast as the mice did?

P22 • Make a silly soup display and draw pictures of the objects in the song. Have a number of different soup bowls to keep each soup rhyme separate.